CHILLOUT MOODS FOR PIANO
a classic collection of 20 laid-back songs

Published by
Wise Publications
8/9 Frith Street, London W1D 3JB, England.

Exclusive Distributors:
Music Sales Limited
Distribution Centre,
Newmarket Road, Bury St. Edmunds,
Suffolk IP33 3YB, England.

Music Sales Pty Limited
120 Rothschild Avenue,
Rosebery, NSW 2018, Australia.

Order No. AM91275
ISBN 0-7119-3509-2
This book © Copyright 2004 by Wise Publications.

Compiled by Lucy Holliday
Music arranged by Derek Jones & Evan Jolly
Music processed by Paul Ewers Music Design
Cover designed by Fresh Lemon
Cover photograph courtesy of Stockbyte
Printed in Malta by Interprint Limited

Your Guarantee of Quality
As publishers, we strive to produce every
book to the highest commercial standards.
The music has been freshly engraved and the
book has been carefully designed to minimise
awkward page turns and to make playing
from it a real pleasure. Particular care has
been given to specifying acid-free, neutral-sized
paper made from pulps which have not been
elemental chlorine bleached. This pulp is from
farmed sustainable forests and was produced
with special regard for the environment.
Throughout, the printing and binding have been
planned to ensure a sturdy, attractive publication
which should give years of enjoyment.
If your copy fails to meet our high standards,
please inform us and we will gladly replace it.

www.musicsales.com

WISE PUBLICATIONS
part of The Music Sales Group
London / New York / Paris / Sydney / Copenhagen / Berlin / Madrid / Tokyo

Almost Blue

Words & Music by Elvis Costello

Slow, freely and with expression

Settle into tempo

♩ = 56 very slow and gentle

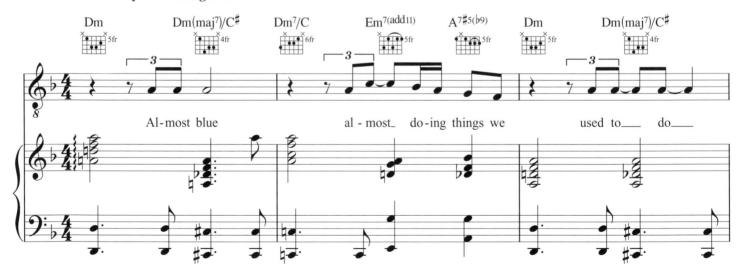

Al-most blue   al - most_ do-ing things we   used to___ do___

there's a boy here and he's___ al-most you,___ al - most,___ all the

things that your eyes once pro-mised I___ see in___

___ his___ too.___ Now your eyes are red from cry - ing,

al - most___ blue.___ Flirt-ing with this dis-as-ter be-

Angel City

Words by Jackie Joyce
Music by Jackie Joyce & The Past Present Organisation

Angel

Words & Music by Sarah McLachlan

arms of_____ the an - gel, fly a - way_____ from here._____

From this dark, cold_____ ho - tel room and the

end - less - ness that you___ fear. You are pulled from the

wreck - age of your si - lent___ re - ve - rie.___ You're in the

arms of _____ the an - gel, may you find _____

some com - fort _____ here. _____

1.

2.

2. So tired of the ___ here. _____

You're in the arms of _____ the

Verse 2:
So tired of the straight line
And everywhere you turn
There's vultures and thieves at your back
And the storm keeps on twisting
You keep on building the lies
That you make up for all that you lack
It don't make no difference
Escape one last time
It's easier to believe
In this sweet madness
Oh this glorious sadness
That brings me to my knees.

In the arms of the angel *etc.*

As Time Goes By

Words & Music by Herman Hupfeld

must get down to earth at times, re - lax, re - lieve the ten - sion. And no

mat - ter what the pro - gress, or what may yet be proved, the sim - ple facts of life are such they

a tempo ♩ = 82

can - not be re - moved. You must re - mem - ber this:__ a kiss is__ still a kiss, a

sigh is just a sigh; the fun - da - ment - al things_____ ap - ply_

as time goes by.___   And___

when two lov-ers woo,___   they still say "I love you,"___   on
*2° Instrumental til ***

that you can re-ly,___   no mat-ter___ what the fu-ture___ brings,___

as time goes by.

But For Now

Words & Music by Robert Dorough

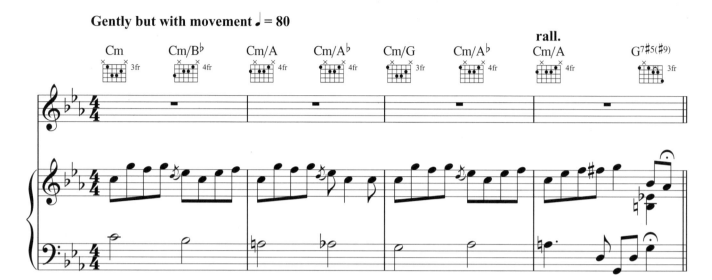

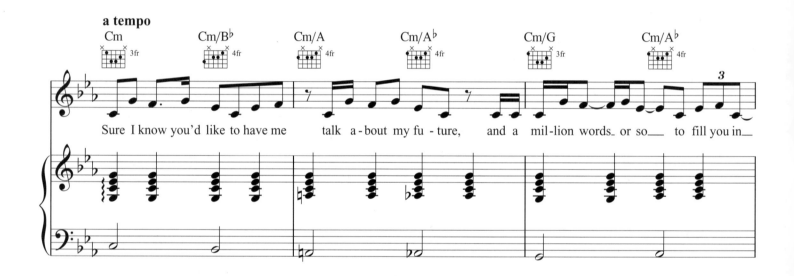

kiss you＿ my dar - ling then once more, once more.

But for

now＿＿＿ let me say I love＿ you＿ la - ter

27

First Time

Words & Music by Beverley Knight & Chris Martin

Rea - son needs no voice, when you know it's true.___ But,
do I let you go? It's still un - clear.___ But,

oh,_____ we make our love a - gain,____ And oh,____
oh,_____ good sense has__ gone to__ waste,____ And oh,____

_____ it's ea - sy__ to pre - tend.___ There's
_____ it fades in__ your em - brace.___ I

so_____ much plea - sure__ through this__ pain.___ I
know_____ what keeps me__ in this__ place.___ Your

29

hard to__ find._ My will is weak__ 'cause my soul's re - signed._ It's like I'm

I'm see-ing you_____ for the first__ time._ I try to speak__

first____ time.__ It's like I'm see - ing you_____ for the

first___ time._ It's like I'm__ see - ing_ you____ for the first____ time.__

The Closest Thing To Crazy

Words & Music by Mike Batt

1. How can I think__ I'm stand - ing strong yet
2. How can you make__ me fall a - part_____ then

feel the air__ be - neath__ my feet?_____
break my fall__ with lov - ing lies?_____

How can hap - pi - ness feel so wrong?
It's so ea - sy to break a heart.

How can mi - se - ry feel so sweet?
It's so ea - sy to close your eyes.

How can you let___ me watch___ you sleep then
How can you treat___ me like a child___ yet

break my dreams___ the way___ you do?_____
like a child___ I yearn___ for you?_____

Help Yourself

Words & Music by Amy Winehouse, Freddy James, Larry Stock & James Hogarth

Humble Me

Words & Music by Kevin Breit

out on a limb,___ gone too far,___ I broke down at the side of the road.___
Ba-by Te-re-sa, she's got your eyes,___ I see you___ all___ the time. When she

I Had A Dream

Words & Music by John B. Sebastian

Freely ♪ = 104 (Gospel Feel)

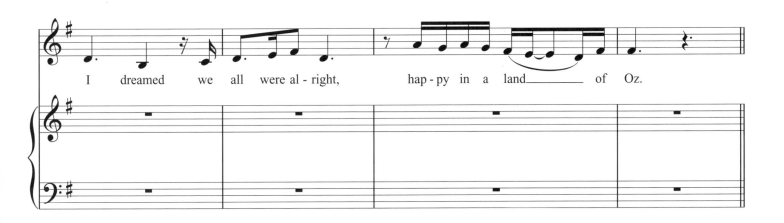

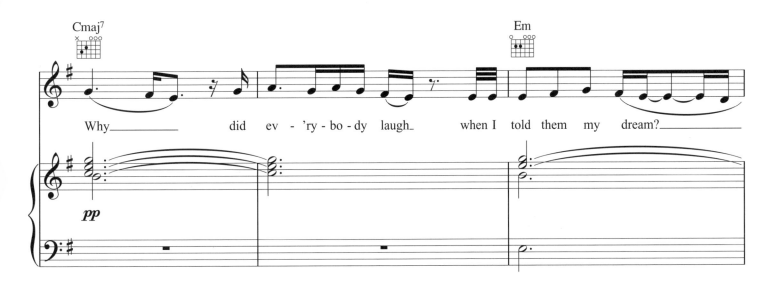

all I re-mem-ber is a feel-ing_____ of sor-row, but as

I re-call,_____ the rest will just fol-low._____

Mmmm._____ I had a dream last_ night.

What a love-ly dream_ it was. I dreamed we

Last Thing On My Mind

Words & Music by Ronan Keating & Stephen Robson

you tried to talk it through.

GIRL:

Now I see it so clear - ly:

BOY:

So I wan-na tell you I'm sor -

we're to-geth-er but liv - ing sep-'rate lives.

-ry. Ba-by, I can't find the words but if I

55

59

I Threw It All Away

Words & Music by Bob Dylan

Once I held_____ him in my_____ arms._____

no chords throughout guitar solo
(implied chords in brackets)

Love_____ is all there is,_____ it makes the world_____ go 'round._____

Love is on - ly love,_____ it can't_____ be de-nied._____

No mat-ter what_ you think a-bout it you won't be a - ble to do__ with-out

it. Take__ a tip from one who's tried.__

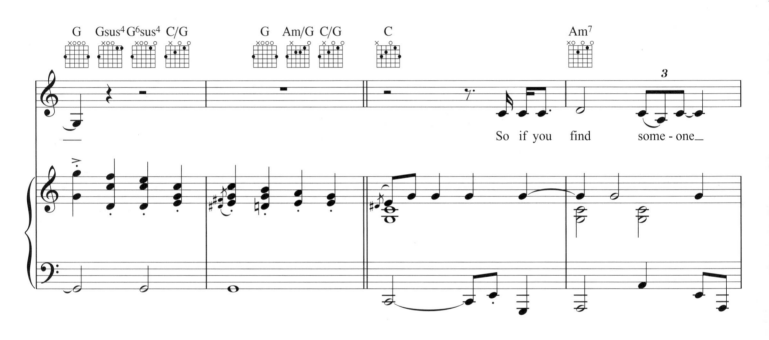

So if you find some-one__

who gives you all of their love__ take it to your

Slip Away

Words & Music by David Bowie

They slip a - way.___ Don't for - get___ to keep_ your head___ warm.

Twin - kle twin - kle Un - cle Floyd.___ Watch - ing all the world_ and

war torn. How I won - der where you are.___ Oh._____

Sail - ing ov - er Co - ney Is - land, twin - kle, twin - kle Un - cle Floyd._

Teach Me Tonight

Words by Sammy Cahn
Music by Gene De Paul

Did you say I've__ got a

Time Enough For Tears

Words & Music by Bono, Gavin Friday & Maurice Seezer

win - ter's sun.___ Don't tell___ me you're leav - ing, we can

(2.) moon___ is milk___ and the

*3° instrumental til ***

hide_ in the eve - ning. It's get-ting dar - ker_ than it should. If we_

sky_where it spilt, it's ma - gic and we all need to be - lieve we can_

read___ the leaves___ as they blow in the breeze_

wake___ in the dream, not as hard as it seems,_

would it stop us now___ my___ love? Time___ e -

you know it's hard - er to leave.___ Time___ e -

89

What The World Needs Now Is Love

Words by Hal David
Music by Burt Bacharach

ev - 'ry - one.

loco

Piano solo

Whenever I Say Your Name

Words & Music by Sting

When - ev - er I say your name, no mat - ter how long it takes, one day we'll be to - geth - er.

When - ev - er I say your name, let there be no mis - take, that day will last for - ev - er.

What A Little Moonlight Can Do

Words & Music by Harry Woods

Ooh - ooh - ooh,___ what a lit-tle moon-light can do___

Ooh - ooh - ooh,___ what a lit-tle moon-light can

do to you.___ You're in love___

your heart's a flut-ter,_____ all day long___ you on-ly stut-ter_____ 'cause

your poor___ tongue just will not ut-ter the words, "I love you."

when you have kissed her is ooh - ooh - OOH   what a lit-tle moon-light can

do!

Piano solo

ooh - ooh - oohm   what a lit-tle moon-light__ can

do.

Repeat ad lib. to fade

You Don't Know Me

Words & Music by Cindy Walker & Eddy Arnold

Slow jazz ballad (12/8 feel) ♩ = 60

fraid_____ and shy,_____ I let my chance go by,

a chance_ that you might love_____ me too.___ You give_____ your_____

hand to me and then_____ you said good-bye.___ I__

watch you walk a-way_____ be-side the luck-y guy.___ You

ne-ver, ne-ver know the one who loves you so, well you don't___ know_ me._____

You Don't Know My Name

Words & Music by Alicia Keys, Kanye West, Harold Lilly, J. R. Bailey,
Melvin Kent & Ken Williams

I'm sayin' he don't even know what he's doin' to me.

I'm feelin' all crazy inside, I'm feeling like... oh, ooh._____

Doin' more than I've ev - er done____ for

know it?

No, no, no, no, no,___ no,

no.___ Will you ev - er know it?

Spoken section: see block lyric

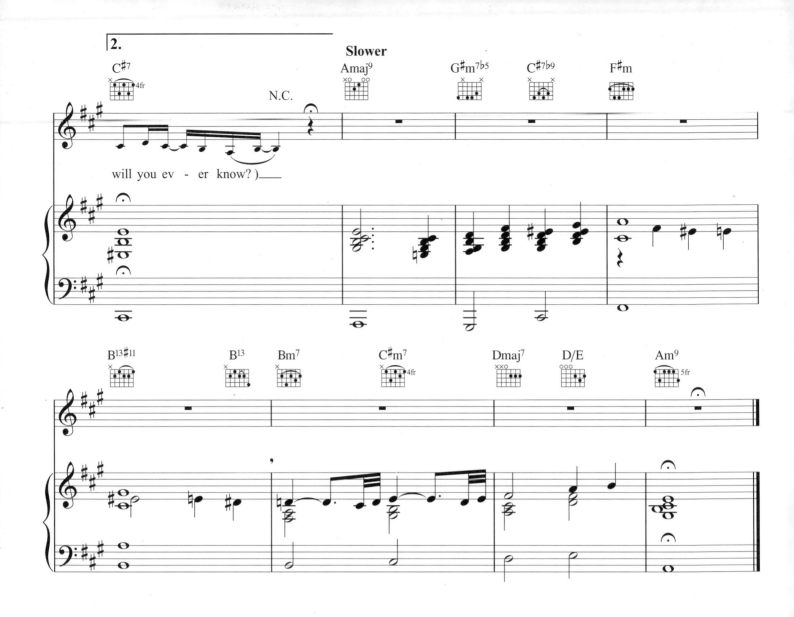

Spoken section:
Well I might have to just go ahead and call this boy.
Hello?
Can I speak to...to Michael? Oh, hey how you doin'?
Uh, I feel kinda silly doin this but, uh,
This is the waitress from the coffee house on 39th from Lenox.
You know the one with the braids?
Yeah. Well I see you on Wednesdays all the time.
You come in every Wednesday on your lunch break, I think.
And you always order the special...with the hot chocolate.
My manager be trippin' and stuff talkin' 'bout we gotta use water, but...
I always use some milk and cream for you, 'cause...
I think you kinda sweet.
Anyway, you always got on some fly blue suit
And your cufflinks is shining all bright.
So what you doin'?
Oh work?
Yeah that's interestin'...
Look man, I mean, I don't wanna waste your time but...
I know girls don't usually do this,
But I was wonderin' if maybe we could get together
Outside the restaurant one day?
You know 'cause I do look a lot different outside my work clothes and...
I mean we could just go across the street to the park, right here...
Wait, hold up, my... my cell phone's breakin' up, hold up...
Can you hear me now?
Yeah. So what day did you say?
Oh yeah. Thursday's perfect, man.